COMPLETE GUIDE TO SHRIMP FARMING

Expert Techniques, Sustainable Practices, And Profit Strategies For Successful Aquaculture

GIOVANNI MALAKAI

© [2024] [Giovanni Malakai]. All rights reserved.

Except for brief quotations included in critical reviews and certain other noncommercial uses allowed by copyright law, no part of this publication may be reproduced, distributed, or transmitted in any form or by any means, including photocopying, recording, or other electronic or mechanical methods, without the publisher's prior written permission. Write to the publisher at the address below, addressing your letter to the "Attention: Permissions Coordinator," requesting permission.

DISCLAIMER

This book's content is solely intended for informational and educational purposes. The author and publisher of this book make no express or implied representations or warranties of any kind regarding the completeness, accuracy, reliability, suitability, or availability of the information, products, services, or related graphics contained in it, even though every effort has been made to ensure their accuracy and dependability. You consequently absolutely assume all risk associated with any reliance you may have on such material.

The author's own experiences and studies serve as the foundation for the techniques and procedures covered in this book. They might not be appropriate for every circumstance or person. Before putting any advice or recommendations from this book into practice, readers should use their own discretion and take into account their unique situation. Consulting with qualified professionals who specialize in veterinary care and animal management is always a good idea. Any direct, indirect, incidental or consequential damages resulting from using or relying on the material in this book are disclaimed by the author and publisher. Any decisions made by the reader based on the information presented herein are at their own risk.

TABLE OF CONTENTS

CHAPTER ONE 13
INTRODUCTION TO SHRIMP FARMING 13
- KNOWING THE FUNDAMENTALS OF SHRIMP FARMING 13
- ADVANTAGES OF OPERATING A SHRIMP FARMING BUSINESS 15
- TOOLS AND EQUIPMENT NEEDED FOR SHRIMP FARMING 17
- IMPORTANT ELEMENTS FOR SUCCESSFUL SHRIMP FARMING 19
- FREQUENTLY HELD MYTHS REGARDING SHRIMP FARMING 21

CHAPTER TWO 23
BEGINNING 23
- CHOOSING THE RIGHT SHRIMP SPECIES 23
- SELECTING THE IDEAL SITE FOR YOUR FARM 24
- PUTTING UP THE INFRASTRUCTURE FOR YOUR SHRIMP FARM 25
- RECOGNIZING WATER QUALITY AND MANAGEMENT 27
- PURCHASING THE FIRST SHRIMP STOCK 28

CHAPTER THREE 31
FARMING METHODS 31
- MONITORING AND UPKEEP OF WATER QUALITY 31
- HANDLING NUTRITION AND FEEDING IN SHRIMP 32
- PREVENTION OF ILLNESSES AND MANAGEMENT OF HEALTH 34
- TRACKING GROWTH AND TIMING HARVESTING 35
- THE BEST METHODS FOR SUSTAINABLE SHRIMP FARMING 36

CHAPTER FOUR 39
ENVIRONMENTAL ASPECTS TO TAKE INTO ACCOUNT 39
- SUSTAINABLE METHODS FOR SHRIMP FARMING 39

- EVALUATION OF ENVIRONMENTAL IMPACT AND MITIGATION 40
- STRATEGIES FOR RECYCLING AND WASTE MANAGEMENT 42
- ECO-FRIENDLY INNOVATIONS IN SHRIMP FARMING 43
- ADHERENCE TO THE REGULATIONS 44

CHAPTER FIVE 45
- SALES AND MARKETING 45
  - ANALYSIS AND RESEARCH OF THE SHRIMP PRODUCT MARKET 45
  - HOW TO PACKAGE AND BRAND YOUR SHRIMP PRODUCTS 46
  - DISTRIBUTION PLANS AND SALES CHANNELS 47
  - STRATEGIES FOR SHRIMP PRODUCT PRICING 49
  - TECHNIQUES FOR ENGAGING AND RETAINING CUSTOMERS 50

CHAPTER SIX 53
- MONEY HANDLING 53
  - COST ANALYSIS AND BUDGETING FOR SHRIMP FARMING 53
  - FORECASTING REVENUE AND PROFIT MARGINS 54
  - INVESTMENT POSSIBILITIES AND SOURCES OF FUNDING 56
  - STRATEGIES FOR FINANCIAL RISK MANAGEMENT 57
  - ACCOUNTING AND RECORD-KEEPING PROCEDURES 59

CHAPTER SEVEN 61
- GROWING YOUR SHRIMP FARM 61
  - STRATEGIES FOR SHRIMP FARM EXPANSION 61
  - PARTNERSHIPS AND OUTSOURCING CHOICES 62
  - HELP WITH HIRING AND DEVELOPING A TEAM 64
  - TECHNIQUES FOR MANAGING INVENTORY 65
  - PLANNING YOUR FINANCES FOR GROWTH 66

CHAPTER EIGHT 69

FAQS & TROUBLESHOOTING 69

- TYPICAL PROBLEMS AND DIFFICULTIES IN SHRIMP FARMING 69
- SOLVING ISSUES WITH WATER QUALITY 70
- TAKING CARE OF DISEASE EPIDEMICS IN SHRIMP FARMS 71
- MANAGING VARIATIONS IN DEMAND AND MARKET 72
- FREQUENTLY ASKED QUESTIONS (FAQS) REGARDING THE 73

CHAPTER NINE 75

UPCOMING DEVELOPMENTS AND TRENDS 75

- NEW TECHNOLOGY IN SHRIMP AGRICULTURE 75
- MARKET OPPORTUNITIES AND INDUSTRY TRENDS 76
- SUSTAINABLE METHODS FOR SHRIMP FARMING IN THE FUTURE 78
- INITIATIVES FOR EDUCATION AND TRAINING 79
- OPPORTUNITIES FOR GLOBAL SHRIMP FARMING GROWTH 81

CHAPTER TEN 83

PARTICIPATION IN THE COMMUNITY 83

- PARTNERSHIPS AND COOPERATIONS WITH LOCAL COMMUNITIES .. 83
- SOCIAL ACCOUNTABILITY AND ECOLOGICAL GUARDIANSHIP 84
- OUTREACH PROGRAMS FOR EDUCATION CONCERNING SHRIMP FARMING 85
- PROMOTING THE CREATION OF JOBS AND LOCAL ECONOMIES 87
- DEVELOPING TRUSTING PARTNERSHIPS WITH STAKEHOLDERS 88

ABOUT THE BOOK

A thorough book that explores the complex world of shrimp farming, "Complete Guide to Shrimp Farming" provides both novice and experienced shrimp farmers with priceless tips and techniques. The fundamental goal of this book is to give readers the skills and information they need to succeed in the fast-paced world of shrimp farming.

The trip starts with a thorough examination of the principles of shrimp farming, educating readers on the many advantages it presents as a successful commercial endeavor. Every facet is carefully covered to guarantee a strong foundation, from comprehending the necessary tools and equipment to identifying the critical success variables.

As you proceed, the guide walks you through important decisions like which shrimp species to choose, where to put your farm, and how to build a strong agricultural infrastructure. To achieve the best harvest results, managing water quality takes center stage, along with insights into managing nutrition, preventing illness, and tracking growth.

Modern shrimp farming places a high priority on environmental concerns, and this book doesn't hold back when discussing eco-friendly innovations, waste management techniques, sustainable methods, and environmental impact assessments. To maintain moral and lawful operations, regulatory compliance is also prioritized.

The book delves further into market research, branding, packaging; sales channels, price strategies, and consumer engagement tactics specifically designed for shrimp goods. Marketing and sales strategies are critical to the success of any firm.

Another important topic that is thoroughly covered is financial management, which includes risk management, investment opportunities, budgeting, revenue forecasting, and strong accounting procedures that are necessary for long-term financial viability.

Strategic planning is necessary for scaling a shrimp farm, and this guide offers priceless insights into partnerships, financial planning, team building, inventory management, and expansion strategies.

Shrimp farming may inevitably present difficulties. To provide farmers with useful answers and information, the troubleshooting area covers frequent problems, water quality issues, disease outbreaks, market changes, and FAQs.

To keep ahead of the curve in a field that is changing quickly, the book looks ahead at future developments and trends in shrimp farming. It does this by highlighting new technology, market trends, sustainable practices, educational programs, and chances for international expansion.

Sustainable shrimp farming practices necessitate community engagement and social responsibility. The guide promotes partnerships with nearby communities, environmental conservation, educational outreach initiatives, and building strong relationships with stakeholders for growth and mutual benefit.

"Complete Guide to Shrimp Farming" offers a comprehensive strategy that includes technical know-how, moral business conduct, and strategic business acumen for successful and sustainable endeavors. It is more than simply a handbook; rather, it is a road map for success in the booming field of shrimp aquaculture.

CHAPTER ONE

INTRODUCTION TO SHRIMP FARMING

KNOWING THE FUNDAMENTALS OF SHRIMP FARMING

Growing shrimp is a complex business that needs a firm grasp of several fundamental concepts. You must first understand the fundamentals of aquaculture, which is the regulated rearing of aquatic organisms like shrimp. This entails understanding the shrimp life cycle, from the hatchery to the grow-out stages, as well as the environmental requirements for each stage. It is essential to comprehend the characteristics of water quality, including temperature, pH, and oxygen content, to sustain a robust shrimp farm. To maximize output, you'll also need to understand the many varieties of shrimp, their rates of growth, and the nutrients they need.

Furthermore, in shrimp farming, knowledge of pond management and preparation is essential. This includes choosing appropriate ground for ponds, tilling the ground, and making sure there is enough water and drainage. Regular monitoring of feeding schedules, stocking densities, and water quality are all part of pond management. To shield shrimp against infections, it also includes biosecurity precautions and disease prevention techniques. Beginners can more successfully traverse the challenges of shrimp farming and improve their chances of success by being aware of these fundamental elements.

Furthermore, for the best possible shrimp growth and productivity, one must become proficient in shrimp farming techniques such as water exchange, aeration, and feeding procedures. By eliminating waste materials and restoring oxygen levels, water exchange contributes to the preservation of water quality. The proper oxygenation provided by aeration systems is essential to the survival and growth of shrimp. To promote healthy shrimp development, feeding tactics comprise giving shrimp balanced diets high in proteins, vitamins, and minerals. Furthermore, by putting good record-keeping and data analysis practices into place, farmers may monitor performance metrics and make deft judgments for ongoing shrimp farming venture improvement.

ADVANTAGES OF OPERATING A SHRIMP FARMING BUSINESS

As a business endeavor, shrimp farming has many benefits that make it a desirable choice for entrepreneurs. Its tremendous potential for profitability is one of the main advantages, particularly given the rising demand for seafood around the world. Shrimp is a well-liked seafood option that fetches high prices in markets all around the world. For shrimp farmers who can effectively handle the production and marketing components, this results in substantial financial prospects. In addition, year-round production offered by shrimp farming lowers the risks associated with seasonality and offers a consistent source of income.

Shrimp farming can also be customized to fit a range of scales, from small-scale businesses to major commercial companies, taking into account different investment amounts and corporate objectives. Additionally, it provides a range of production methods that are flexible, such as intensive systems like raceways or tanks, conventional pond-based farming, and cutting-edge techniques like recirculating aquaculture systems (RAS). Because of their flexibility, farmers can investigate sustainable practices for long-term sustainability, scale operations in response to market demand, and maximize resource utilization.

Moreover, by generating jobs in rural areas and assisting auxiliary businesses like feed manufacturing, equipment manufacturing, and processing facilities, shrimp farming promotes economic development. To meet the increasing demands of consumers, it also supports food security by offering wholesome protein sources. Furthermore, by using sustainable farming methods, protecting habitats, and managing water resources, shrimp farming may support environmental sustainability objectives. This increases the industry's attractiveness as a socially and environmentally responsible commercial endeavor.

TOOLS AND EQUIPMENT NEEDED FOR SHRIMP FARMING

Having the appropriate tools and equipment to enable effective operations and guarantee ideal shrimp growth is essential for successful shrimp farming. Ponds or tanks intended for shrimp farming are essential pieces of equipment. They should include liners to preserve the soil, water entry, and outflow systems to circulate the water, and screens to keep out predators and undesirable species. Appropriate aeration apparatus, like diffused aeration systems or paddlewheel aerators, is necessary to keep water oxygen levels sufficient, which is necessary for shrimp respiration and metabolism.

Furthermore, in shrimp farming, technologies for monitoring and management are essential. Monitoring tools for water quality, such as temperature sensors, dissolved oxygen probes, and pH meters, assist farmers in determining the ideal circumstances for shrimp health and in making the required adjustments.

Feeding apparatus, including feeding trays or motorized feeders, guarantees precise and prompt meal distribution, reducing waste and maximizing shrimp nutrient uptake. To effectively manage production operations, farmers can also make use of nets, harvesting equipment, and water testing instruments.

Additionally, shrimp farming relies heavily on biosecurity techniques for disease prevention and management. These could include facilities for new stock quarantine, procedures for staff and equipment decontamination, and surveillance programs to identify early indicators of disease outbreaks.

By putting biosecurity procedures into place, the risk of pathogen introduction and spread is decreased, protecting shrimp populations and agricultural output. Shrimp producers may improve farm performance, reduce hazards, and streamline operations by investing in high-quality tools and equipment.

IMPORTANT ELEMENTS FOR SUCCESSFUL SHRIMP FARMING

The success of shrimp farming operations is largely dependent on several important criteria. Controlling the quality of the water is crucial since shrimp are extremely sensitive to changes in their surroundings. Shrimp growth is encouraged and stress-related problems are reduced when ideal water conditions, such as temperature, pH, salinity, and dissolved oxygen levels, are maintained. The size, depth, and arrangement of a pond or tank should be carefully considered as this affects the overall productivity of the farm by facilitating effective water circulation, waste management, and stocking densities.

Moreover, disease control plans are necessary to reduce health hazards associated with shrimp farming. Implementing biosecurity measures, tracking diseases, and performing routine health assessments all contribute to preventing the entry and spread of infections.

To establish a clean environment that promotes shrimp health, farmers should implement best practices for sanitation, hygiene, and water treatment. Enhancing farm resistance against common diseases can also be accomplished by initiating vaccination programs or choosing disease-resistant shrimp species.

Furthermore, effective feed management is essential to the profitability of shrimp farming. Optimizing feed conversion, decreasing waste, and facilitating effective nutrient use are all facilitated by providing nutritionally balanced meals that are customized to the life phases and growth requirements of shrimp. To optimize shrimp performance and reduce production costs, farmers should take into account variables including feed composition, feeding frequency, pellet size, and feeding strategies. To maximize feeding techniques for increased profitability and sustainability, it is helpful to monitor feed consumption, growth rates, and feed conversion ratios.

FREQUENTLY HELD MYTHS REGARDING SHRIMP FARMING

Despite the potential advantages, there are a lot of myths about shrimp farming that can mislead prospective growers. A prevalent misperception is that raising shrimp is an easy and low-maintenance activity. In actuality, success in shrimp farming demands a great deal of knowledge, money, and attention to detail. It entails intricate management techniques that call for ongoing learning and condition adaptability, such as illness prevention, feed management, and regulation of water quality.

The idea that shrimp aquaculture harms the environment is another fallacy. While improperly run shrimp farms can harm the environment, sustainable farming methods can reduce ecological footprint and increase ecological footprint. Shrimp farming poses some environmental concerns that can be reduced by employing water treatment techniques, recirculating aquaculture systems (RAS), and best management practices (BMPs). In line with international conservation objectives, sustainable shrimp farming projects prioritize biodiversity preservation, water resource management, and habitat conservation.

Furthermore, it's a common misperception that shrimp farming can only be done in coastal regions with access to saltwater. While there are inherent benefits to raising shrimp near the ocean, it is also possible to grow shrimp inland utilizing freshwater or brackish water sources with the right infrastructure and management techniques. The geographical potential for shrimp farming has increased due to advancements in closed-system aquaculture, pond design, and water treatment technology. This has allowed inland farmers to enter the market and diversify their production locations. Promoting informed decision-making and sustainable growth in the shrimp farming industry requires an understanding of and commitment to debunking these myths.

CHAPTER TWO

BEGINNING

CHOOSING THE RIGHT SHRIMP SPECIES

For your shrimp farming endeavor to be successful, selecting the appropriate species of shrimp is essential. Start by learning about the many species that are suitable for farming in your area. Take into account variables such as growth rate, disease resistance, salinity tolerance, water temperature, and market demand. Indian white shrimp, huge tiger prawns, and Pacific white shrimp are common shrimp species farmed.

After you've located possible species, assess what they need in terms of environmental factors, eating patterns, and water quality.

While some species favor freshwater or marine settings, others flourish in brackish water. Examine the species you have picked, their suitability for your agricultural infrastructure, and the availability of resources such as feed and larvae.

Lastly, to gain knowledge about the ideal species for your particular region and objectives, speak with knowledgeable farmers or aquaculture specialists in the area. To assess the viability of shrimp, think about starting with a small batch and modifying your farming techniques as necessary. The key to a productive and successful farming operation is choosing the appropriate species of shrimp.

SELECTING THE IDEAL SITE FOR YOUR FARM

The long-term viability and output of your shrimp farm depend on your choice of site. Assessing water quality metrics like temperature, salinity, pH, and oxygen concentration should come first. To ensure that your shrimp farm fits the requirements for shrimp farming and that your stock grows and is healthy, conduct extensive testing and surveys.

Take into account environmental elements such as water depth, tidal changes, and pollution or contaminant exposure. Select a site where there are fewer chances of flooding, severe weather, or industrial pollution that could affect the health and productivity of shrimp. To keep the water quality in your farm tanks or ponds at its best, you must have access to clean water and install suitable drainage systems.

Assess logistical factors as well, like labor availability, market accessibility, infrastructure for transportation, and regulatory compliance. To find out what licenses, permits, and zoning restrictions apply to shrimp farming in the area you have selected, speak with the local government. Selecting an appropriate site is essential for establishing a prosperous and long-lasting shrimp farming enterprise.

PUTTING UP THE INFRASTRUCTURE FOR YOUR SHRIMP FARM

After deciding on a good site, it's time to build up the infrastructure needed for shrimp farming. Based on the size and scope of your enterprise, start by planning and building ponds or tanks. To keep predators and unlawful access at bay, take into account elements like pond depth, surface area, water circulation systems, and fence.

Install aeration devices to keep the water's oxygen levels at ideal levels—this is important for the health and growth of shrimp. Install systems for water filtration and treatment to eliminate contaminants and uphold water quality requirements. Purchase the necessary equipment, such as feeders, aerators, pumps, and monitoring systems, based on whether you practice extensive, semi-intensive, or intense farming.

Create feeding schedules and find premium feed that is appropriate for the species and growth stages of your shrimp. Create a thorough management plan that addresses illness prevention, stocking density, harvesting methods, and water quality monitoring. Educate your employees on biosecurity precautions, appropriate farming techniques, and emergency response protocols. A well-thought-out and productive farming infrastructure must be established to maximize shrimp production and profitability.

RECOGNIZING WATER QUALITY AND MANAGEMENT

To guarantee the best possible growth, health, and production in shrimp farming, water quality management is essential. To start, test the water frequently for various factors like temperature, salinity, pH, dissolved oxygen, ammonia, nitrite, and nitrate levels. To keep the perfect environment for shrimp, keep a careful eye on these factors and make any required modifications.

Install recirculation or water exchange systems to regulate water quality parameters and reduce environmental effects. Handle feed supplies correctly to avoid water contamination and nutrient imbalances. To keep the water clear and eliminate solids—which is essential for shrimp visibility and feeding efficiency—use mechanical or natural filtering techniques.

Put biosecurity measures in place to stop infections from entering and spreading throughout your shrimp farm.

Clean equipment, quarantine fresh inventory and keep an eye out for any indications of illness outbreaks. Create a backup plan in case of water emergencies such as chemical spills, oxygen shortages, or algae blooms. For shrimp farming operations to be sustainable and profitable, one must understand the concepts of water quality management.

PURCHASING THE FIRST SHRIMP STOCK

Purchasing healthy and disease-free shrimp stock is essential to getting your farming business off to a good start. Start by obtaining shrimp larvae or juveniles from reliable hatcheries or vendors who have demonstrated their ability to generate robust and healthy stock. Make sure there are no infections, parasites, or genetic anomalies in the stock.

To reduce stress and death, carefully transfer the shrimp stock to your farm using the right containers and techniques. As the stock gets used to the farm environment, gradually increases or decreases the water conditions and feeding schedules.

Throughout the acclimatization stage, keep a close eye on the shrimp's health and behavior to spot any problems early.

Put in place quarantine procedures to keep new animals apart from current populations and stop the spread of possible illnesses. Keep an eye on growth rates, survival rates, and feed conversion ratios to evaluate how well your initial shrimp stock performed. To achieve the best outcomes, adjust stocking densities and management techniques in collaboration with knowledgeable aquaculture experts or consultants. To achieve a successful farming operation, acquiring and managing early shrimp stock involves meticulous planning, close attention to detail, and continuous monitoring.

CHAPTER THREE

FARMING METHODS

MONITORING AND UPKEEP OF WATER QUALITY

To provide a healthy and productive environment for the shrimp, monitoring and maintaining the quality of the water is an essential part of shrimp farming. It entails routinely monitoring and controlling variables including the water's pH, dissolved oxygen content, temperature, salinity, and ammonia content.

Beginners should purchase quality testing kits and routinely check these factors to maintain the best possible water quality. To sustain shrimp respiration, pH levels should preferably be kept between 7.5 and 8.5 and dissolved oxygen levels should be greater than 5 mg/L. Controlling the temperature is crucial; for the majority of shrimp species, a range of 25 to 30 degrees Celsius is usually advised. Salinity requirements can differ throughout farmed species; freshwater shrimp require lower salinity levels than marine shrimp.

Shrimp can become poisoned by high ammonia levels, thus it's best to keep them low.

To preserve water quality, appropriate systems for filtration and water exchange should be in place in addition to routine monitoring. While water exchange helps replenish oxygen and dilute toxic compounds, filtration aids in the removal of trash and waste products. Ultimately, as water quality has a direct impact on shrimp health, growth rates, and total productivity, maintaining ideal water quality is essential to a shrimp farm's success.

HANDLING NUTRITION AND FEEDING IN SHRIMP

Shrimp farming involves crucial issues like as feeding and nutrition management, which have a direct impact on growth rates, health, and total output. Novices should be aware of the dietary needs of shrimp and adjust their feeding techniques accordingly.

A diet rich in proteins, lipids, carbs, vitamins, and minerals is necessary for shrimp. Various formulas of commercial shrimp feeds are available to fulfill these dietary requirements. Novice shrimp farmers should adhere to suggested feeding guidelines and select feeds that are suitable for the species of shrimp they are farming.

Carefully monitoring feeding frequencies and amounts is necessary to avoid overfeeding or underfeeding. Underfeeding can impede growth and lower overall productivity, while overfeeding can cause problems with water quality because of excessive waste. When feeding shrimp, it's critical to watch their activity to make sure they're eating the feed properly.

To improve nutritional diversity, supplemental feeds like natural feeds (algae, plankton) can be added to the diet in addition to commercial feeds. Optimizing farm profitability, reducing stress, and boosting shrimp development are all dependent on proper feeding and nutrition management.

PREVENTION OF ILLNESSES AND MANAGEMENT OF HEALTH

To stop outbreaks and maintain a healthy stock, disease prevention, and health management are crucial in the shrimp farming industry. Novices should take stringent biosecurity precautions and routinely check the health of their shrimp.

Quarantining new stock, cleaning facilities and equipment, and regulating water quality factors to lessen stress and disease susceptibility are examples of biosecurity practices. It is important to get regular checkups to identify any early warning symptoms of illness.

Infections with bacteria, viruses (such as the White Spot Syndrome Virus), and parasites are common diseases affecting shrimp. Implementing appropriate hygiene measures, getting vaccinated when accessible, and managing water quality are examples of prevention strategies.

Rapid identification and treatment are essential in the event of a disease outbreak. It is recommended that novices collaborate closely with veterinary specialists or other seasoned experts to determine the underlying cause of the illness and establish suitable treatment measures. To keep the shrimp population healthy, disease prevention and health management are continual duties that call for diligence and preventive measures.

TRACKING GROWTH AND TIMING HARVESTING

To optimize profits and guarantee high-quality products, shrimp farming requires careful monitoring of growth and time of harvesting. Novices should keep a close eye on the growth rates of shrimp and schedule their harvests according to shrimp size and market demands.

Shrimp growth characteristics including size, weight, and developmental phases are monitored. The best time to harvest is determined in part by this information. When shrimp reach marketable sizes, which vary by species but usually range from 20 to 30 grams, they should be picked.

The right timing of harvesting is essential to prevent too-developed shrimp, which can lower their quality and market value. To preserve freshness and quality, novices should organize their harvesting operations to align with periods of high market demand. They should also make sure that collected shrimp are handled and transported properly.

For shrimp growers, higher yields, better product quality, and increased profitability are all a result of proper growth monitoring and harvesting time. Making educated decisions about harvesting schedules and product offerings requires keeping up with consumer preferences and market trends.

THE BEST METHODS FOR SUSTAINABLE SHRIMP FARMING

Putting best practices for sustainable shrimp farming into practice is essential to ensuring long-term viability, minimizing environmental effects, and conserving resources. Beginners should embrace ecological balance and responsible aquaculture by implementing sustainable farming methods and practices.

Essential methods encompass conserving water using optimal utilization and repurposing, reducing refuse and contamination via appropriate waste-handling techniques, and fostering biodiversity in agricultural environments.

Systems such as integrated multi-trophic aquaculture (IMTA) can be used to make use of byproducts and foster beneficial interactions between various species.

Moreover, sustainable shrimp farming is facilitated by the ethical procurement of feeds and inputs, strategic farm placement to reduce environmental effects, and compliance with legal requirements and certifications. To stay current with industry innovations and best practices, farmers must get ongoing education and training in sustainable methods.

Shrimp farmers can guarantee the long-term sustainability of their businesses, meet customer demand for eco-friendly products, and help environmental protection by making sustainability a priority. Sustainable shrimp farming methods are advantageous for aquaculture communities' social and economic facets as well as the environment.

CHAPTER FOUR

ENVIRONMENTAL ASPECTS TO TAKE INTO ACCOUNT

SUSTAINABLE METHODS FOR SHRIMP FARMING

To ensure both a profitable business and a healthy ecosystem, sustainable shrimp farming procedures are essential. The selection of the place is the most important factor.

The best places have acceptable water quality, comfortable temperatures, and little pollution. It's critical to implement responsible stocking densities after the place has been selected. Disease outbreaks and water contamination can result from overstocking. Shrimp health and growth depend on proper water management, which includes routinely checking the water's quality and preserving the ideal amount of oxygen in it.

An additional crucial component of sustainable shrimp farming is the use of environmentally acceptable feed sources. Choose feeds derived from sustainable sources, such as fishmeal that has been ethically sourced or plant-based ingredients. This enhances the quality of the shrimp produced while also lessening the impact on the environment. Furthermore, the implementation of integrated farming systems can optimize resource usage and reduce waste, for example, by merging aquaculture or agriculture with shrimp farming.

Sustainability is further enhanced by applying techniques such as encouraging biodiversity in the farm environment, putting in place organic waste recycling systems, and implementing biosecurity measures to prevent disease outbreaks. Shrimp growers may assure long-term profitability while reducing adverse effects on the environment by adhering to these sustainable methods.

EVALUATION OF ENVIRONMENTAL IMPACT AND MITIGATION

It's imperative to carry out a thorough environmental impact assessment (EIA) before starting a shrimp farm.

This assessment aids in the development of mitigation strategies by assessing potential environmental concerns. Considerations such as waste management, habitat disturbance, and water quality are carefully evaluated to reduce negative impacts on the local ecology.

Putting into practice efficient water management techniques is one of the main mitigation options. This entails routinely checking the pH, dissolved oxygen, and nutrient levels, among other water quality metrics. Efficient techniques for disposing of waste, like biofilters and sedimentation ponds, aid in lowering the amount of contaminants that are released into natural water bodies from farms.

Further reducing environmental effects include erecting buffer zones surrounding the farm, preserving mangrove ecosystems where feasible, and utilizing environmentally friendly farm equipment such as recirculating aquaculture systems (RAS). Maintaining ongoing improvements in environmental performance requires regular monitoring and adherence to legal requirements.

STRATEGIES FOR RECYCLING AND WASTE MANAGEMENT

Sustainable shrimp farming requires efficient waste management. By putting methods in place to reduce, reuse, and recycle waste materials, operational efficiency is increased while the environmental impact is minimized. To start, eliminate excess feed and fecal matter in aquatic bodies by optimizing feed management procedures. To reduce waste, use automated feeding systems or feed trays.

Furthermore, implementing biosecurity practices such as pond preparation, consistent water exchange, and probiotic use can improve the farm ecosystem's ability to recycle nutrients and break down waste. Waste can be transformed into nutrients that shrimp and other aquatic species can benefit from by using natural biological processes, such as the microbial decomposition of organic debris.

Additionally, investigate cutting-edge technology like sludge digesters, which turn organic waste into biogas for energy production, and bioremediation ponds, in which helpful bacteria break down organic waste. These tactics support the overall sustainability of shrimp farming operations in addition to lowering environmental contamination.

ECO-FRIENDLY INNOVATIONS IN SHRIMP FARMING

Sustainability is considerably enhanced by innovations in environmentally friendly shrimp farming. Shrimp farming is combined with other species, such as fish and seaweed, in integrated multi-trophic aquaculture (IMTA) systems, which creates a symbiotic ecosystem that reduces waste and increases output. Carbon emissions are decreased when renewable energy sources like solar or wind power are used instead of fossil fuels.

Using cutting-edge technologies like resource-saving automated feeding systems and water quality monitoring increases productivity. Putting money into the creation of disease-resistant shrimp varieties lowers the demand for antibiotics and encourages better agricultural methods. Accepting these improvements improves the long-term economic viability of shrimp farming while also helping the environment.

ADHERENCE TO THE REGULATIONS

Respecting legal requirements is essential to sustainable shrimp farming. This entails securing licenses and permits, adhering to regulations regarding water quality, and meeting waste discharge limitations. Regulatory authorities set environmental and safety standards for farms, which are ensured by routine audits and inspections.

Farmers can stay aware and compliant by participating in ongoing education and training on best practices and regulatory updates. To prove compliance and accountability, precise documentation of farming operations, water quality criteria, and waste management procedures must be kept.

CHAPTER FIVE

SALES AND MARKETING

ANALYSIS AND RESEARCH OF THE SHRIMP PRODUCT MARKET

Comprehending market research and analysis is essential for any endeavor involving shrimp farming. Investigate customer preferences, demand-supply dynamics, and competition analysis to start learning about the current market trends. Examine customer behavior in detail to determine target demographics, inclinations, and purchasing trends for shrimp-related goods. Conduct focus groups, and surveys, and use web analytics tools to collect detailed information.

Next, examine the gathered data to find possibilities and gaps in the market. Seek for underutilized markets or new trends that your shrimp products may take advantage of. To create a strategic strategy for entering a market, conduct a SWOT analysis of your strengths, weaknesses, opportunities, and threats. To properly position your shrimp items, take into account elements like pricing, packaging, and promotional techniques based on market research.

After analysis, improve your marketing plans in light of the new information. Create a shrimp product unique selling proposition (USP) that appeals to your target market. Adapt your benefits, features, and marketing messaging to the expectations of the target market. Keep an eye on consumer feedback and market developments to adjust and maximize your marketing efforts for long-term success.

HOW TO PACKAGE AND BRAND YOUR SHRIMP PRODUCTS

Having strong branding and packaging is essential to drawing in and keeping customers for your shrimp goods. Establish your brand identity first, including your mission, values, and unique selling propositions. Craft a captivating brand narrative that appeals to your intended audience and emphasizes the excellence, eco-friendliness, and freshness of your shrimp offerings.

Create visually striking packaging that appeals to customers and represents your brand identity. To keep up with customer tastes and sustainability trends, think about eco-friendly packaging alternatives. To improve the consumer experience, include educational labeling that emphasizes important product qualities, certifications (such as organic or MSC-certified), and cooking instructions.

Ensure that your branding is consistent on all channels—websites, physical stores, and marketing collateral. To increase your brand's visibility and expand your audience, make use of digital marketing platforms including influencer collaborations, email campaigns, and social media. To foster brand advocacy and loyalty, communicate with consumers through interactive content, competitions, and feedback channels.

DISTRIBUTION PLANS AND SALES CHANNELS

Selecting the appropriate distribution networks and sales channels is crucial to successfully reaching your target market. Examine other sales channels, including collaborations with restaurants and food service providers, wholesale to retailers, and direct-to-consumer (DTC) through your website. When choosing sales channels, take into account variables like price, reach, and client preferences.

Create a thorough distribution strategy to guarantee product freshness and on-time delivery. To simplify operations, build a distribution network or collaborate with reputable logistics partners. Use inventory management systems to estimate demand, keep an eye on stock levels, and avoid stockouts and overstocking situations.

Optimize your distribution plans in light of performance indicators and market feedback. To optimize efficiency and satisfy customers, adjust your distribution networks based on market developments, consumer input, and sales statistics. Keep looking for new ways to grow your shrimp farming business and increase sales, such as through e-commerce platforms or foreign markets.

STRATEGIES FOR SHRIMP PRODUCT PRICING

In the shrimp farming industry, competitiveness and profit maximization depend on effective pricing tactics. Perform a pricing analysis, taking into account variables such as production costs, market demand, rival pricing, and consumer perception of value. Establish your price goals, such as increasing market share, optimizing income, or providing value-based pricing.

Use dynamic pricing techniques to modify prices in response to demand patterns, market situations, and promotional events. To encourage recurring business and client loyalty, provide package discounts, loyalty plans, or bundle packages. Think about value-added pricing by emphasizing special features of the product, like premium quality or sustainable practices.

Review and modify your pricing strategy regularly in light of the competitive environment, cost variations, and market dynamics. For pricing decisions to remain flexible and responsive, keep an eye on pricing trends, rival moves, and consumer input.

To improve your price plans for long-term profitability and market success, use tools for pricing optimization or seek advice from professionals in the field.

TECHNIQUES FOR ENGAGING AND RETAINING CUSTOMERS

Establishing trusting bonds with clients and encouraging loyalty is essential for long-term success in the shrimp farming industry. Use consumer engagement techniques to interact with your audience and get insightful data, such as tailored messaging, feedback forms, and loyalty schemes. Use content marketing, email marketing, and social media to interact with customers and provide insightful information about your shrimp goods.

By answering questions quickly, finding effective solutions to problems, and going above and beyond for customers, you may deliver great customer service. To establish credibility and trust with prospective customers, promote client endorsements and reviews. Increase the reach of your business and draw in new clients by utilizing influencer relationships and user-generated content.

Use retention tactics to promote recurring business and enduring client loyalty, such as special offers, product bundles, and subscription services. To determine customer satisfaction levels and pinpoint areas for development, track customer satisfaction indicators like Net Promoter Score (NPS) or customer feedback ratings. Maintaining a devoted client base and fostering business success need you to constantly innovate and modify your customer interaction techniques in response to feedback and market changes.

CHAPTER SIX

MONEY HANDLING

COST ANALYSIS AND BUDGETING FOR SHRIMP FARMING

Cost analysis and budgeting are essential components of running a profitable shrimp farming operation. Assess your initial land, equipment, and infrastructure needs before making any investments. Make a thorough budget that accounts for all of these costs, including one-time expenditures and ongoing costs for things like labor, feed, utilities, and upkeep. To guarantee proper budgeting, do some research and pricing comparisons for the required goods and equipment.

After that, carry out a comprehensive cost analysis to determine how profitable your shrimp farming business is. Include production expenses for labor, disease preventive strategies, feed, and water quality management. To determine the possible revenue, compare these expenses to the shrimp market pricing.

When estimating sales and setting prices for your items, take into account factors such as competition, seasonality, and market demand.

As your shrimp farming business develops, analyze and tweak your cost analysis and budget regularly. Keep a careful eye on your spending to find places where you may cut costs without sacrificing sustainability or quality. Use software and tools for financial management to keep tabs on your income, expenses, and general financial situation. You can maximize profitability and long-term success in shrimp farming by making well-informed judgments and by continuing to take a proactive approach to budgeting and cost analysis.

FORECASTING REVENUE AND PROFIT MARGINS

Planning for future growth and estimating the revenue from shrimp sales depend heavily on revenue forecasting. Analyze demand swings, pricing dynamics, and market trends in the shrimp business first. Take into consideration variables that could affect sales volumes and prices, such as seasonality, consumer preferences, and the state of the economy. To create accurate revenue estimates, consult past data and industry standards.

Take the money from shrimp sales and deduct the cost of production to determine your profit margins. Consider both fixed costs, such as overhead and equipment depreciation, and variable costs, such as labor, feed, and utilities. To reach desired profit margins, establish sales goals and breakeven points. Investigate methods to boost sales, such as broadening your product line, reaching a wider audience, and increasing the effectiveness of your manufacturing process.

Review and modify your profit margin projections and revenue estimates regularly in light of the state of the market and actual sales results. To assess financial performance and pinpoint areas for development, track key performance indicators (KPIs) such as net profit margin, gross profit margin, and return on investment

(ROI). Shrimp farming may enhance its financial sustainability and competitiveness by upholding precise revenue projections and improving profit margins.

INVESTMENT POSSIBILITIES AND SOURCES OF FUNDING

Initiating and growing a shrimp farming business requires looking into investment alternatives and obtaining money. Assessing your capital requirements for equipment purchases, property acquisition, infrastructure development, and operating costs should be your first step. Based on your production objectives, growth strategy, and business plan, decides what kind and how much investment is needed.

Look into financing options that fit your needs both financially and strategically, such as grants, loans, venture capital, and private investors. Create a thorough fundraising proposal that details your project, including a financial forecast, risk analysis, and possible returns on investment.

Draw attention to your experience, competitive advantages, and market analysis to entice lenders or investors.

To find funding opportunities and form strategic alliances, interact with government agencies, financial institutions, industry networks, and investment forums. Maintain openness and regulatory compliance while negotiating advantageous terms and conditions for funding agreements. Shrimp farming might experience faster growth and profitability if you can leverage investment opportunities and secure sufficient cash.

STRATEGIES FOR FINANCIAL RISK MANAGEMENT

Shrimp farming might face significant problems and uncertainties, which can be mitigated by putting appropriate financial risk management measures into practice. Determine and evaluate the risks that could affect financial stability, including market volatility, production hiccups, disease outbreaks, changes in regulations, and natural disasters.

Create backup plans and risk-reduction techniques to reduce possible losses and safeguard your investment.

Experiment with several product lines, markets, and distribution methods to diversify your revenue sources and lessen your reliance on any one source of income. Invest in risk management instruments and insurance coverage to protect against future losses due to crop failure, property damage, liability lawsuits, and company disruptions. To handle unforeseen costs and preserve cash during hard times, set up emergency funds and reserve capital.

Review and update your risk management plans regularly in response to changing market conditions, company trends, and internal issues that impact your shrimp farming operation. Speak with legal professionals, financial advisors, and industry experts to identify hazards and put preventative measures in place to protect your financial well-being. Through the implementation of a proactive financial risk management strategy, shrimp farming can be made more resilient and sustainable.

ACCOUNTING AND RECORD-KEEPING PROCEDURES

The foundation of strong accounting principles and accurate record-keeping is financial management in shrimp farming. Create a methodical record-keeping system to monitor sales, purchases, inventory, income, and expenses, as well as financial activities. Streamline bookkeeping procedures and provide thorough financial reports for analysis and decision-making by using accounting software or tools.

Adopt basic accounting procedures including cash flow management, budget variance analysis, double-entry bookkeeping, and financial statement preparation. Make sure that the reporting requirements, tax laws, and accounting guidelines that apply to shrimp farming activities are followed. To assess profitability and efficiency, maintain thorough records of production parameters, yield statistics, input utilization, and operational performance.

To find inconsistencies, mistakes, or fraud, reconcile bank statements, invoices, receipts, and financial records regularly. To evaluate internal controls, risk exposure, and adherence to financial policies and procedures, conducts recurring audits and financial reviews. To improve skills and expertise in accounting procedures, staff members in charge of financial management should receive training and development. In shrimp farming, you may maximize financial transparency, decision-making, and regulatory compliance by keeping correct records and implementing best accounting practices.

CHAPTER SEVEN
GROWING YOUR SHRIMP FARM
STRATEGIES FOR SHRIMP FARM EXPANSION

Careful planning and execution are necessary when expanding your shrimp farm to guarantee profitability and long-term growth. Diversifying your product line is a crucial tactic. Some examples of this include investigating various shrimp species and introducing supplementary items like sauces for seafood or snacks made with shrimp. This draws in a larger consumer base and expands revenue streams. Additionally, think about reaching out to new customers both domestically and abroad by focusing on specialized markets or utilizing new distribution channels.

Optimizing your production procedures for more productivity and efficiency is an additional tactic. This could entail making investments in new machinery and technology, putting best practices for feed and water optimization into effect, and routinely checking and enhancing the environmental conditions on your farm. You can increase output while upholding quality standards and cutting expenses by optimizing processes.

Additionally, forming strategic alliances and working together can be very helpful in growing your shrimp farm. This includes collaborating with distributors or retailers to gain broader market access, building partnerships with suppliers for reliable input sourcing, and teaming up with research institutions or industry experts for information sharing and innovation. These alliances may provide resources, knowledge, and market intelligence that will accelerate the expansion of your farm.

PARTNERSHIPS AND OUTSOURCING CHOICES

To maximize resources and concentrate on core strengths, it may be a wise strategic decision to outsource some portions of your shrimp farm operations. One choice is to outsource the production of feed to specialized manufacturers, which lowers production costs and risks while guaranteeing high-quality feeds customized to your shrimp's nutritional demands. In a similar vein, using outside companies to manage ponds or check the health of shrimp can improve farm output and disease control.

For the benefit of shrimp farmers, partnerships with processing plants or seafood exporters may also be advantageous. Working together with these organizations gives you access to distribution networks, market knowledge, and value-added processing services that can increase the competitiveness and market reach of your farm. Investigating joint partnerships or strategic alliances with other aquaculture or shrimp farming businesses can also result in the sharing of resources, the sharing of information, and coordinated marketing initiatives for both parties' success and growth.

Furthermore, by contracting with outside organizations or consultants to handle administrative duties like bookkeeping, legal compliance, and marketing campaigns, businesses can guarantee regulatory compliance, expedite processes, and free up internal staff for strategic planning and farm management.

HELP WITH HIRING AND DEVELOPING A TEAM

Developing a knowledgeable and committed staff is essential to your shrimp farm's expansion and success. To start, enlist the help of consultants or hire seasoned aquaculture professionals to help with technical elements, strategic planning, and farm management. To improve farm productivity and sustainability, these specialists may offer insightful advice, educational opportunities, and continuous assistance.

Focus on developing a robust farm staff with competent workers for pond management, feeding operations, and maintenance duties in addition to technological skills. To create a happy workplace, increase productivity, and lower attrition rates, spend money on safety procedures, training initiatives, and employee rewards. Promote cooperation, dialogue, and coordination among team members to maximize efficiency and accomplish shared agricultural objectives.

Additionally, think about using automation and technology in farm operations to enhance productivity and supplement human labor. This could include data analytics tools, sensors for monitoring water quality, and automated feeding systems to give your staff real-time information and help with decision-making for efficient farm management.

TECHNIQUES FOR MANAGING INVENTORY

To meet market demands, minimize waste, and maintain ideal stock levels, effective inventory management is essential. Accurate inventory control of shrimp stocks, feed inventory, equipment, and other farm supplies can be achieved by putting in place inventory control methods such as batch tracking, the FIFO (First In, First Out) method, and frequent stock audits.

Make use of technological tools such as inventory management software to estimate demand, keep track of inventory levels, and automate replenishment procedures. This makes proactive inventory management possible, lowers the likelihood of stockouts or overstocks, and boosts overall operational effectiveness. Build strong ties with your suppliers and bargain for advantageous terms to ensure consistent and timely inventory replenishment.

To maintain shrimp quality and increase shelf life, add quality control techniques and storage procedures. Maintaining the integrity of the product and upholding quality standards requires careful handling, packing, and storage conditions, including temperature control and hygienic procedures.

To maximize agricultural operations, evaluate inventory performance data regularly, look for patterns, and modify inventory tactics as necessary.

PLANNING YOUR FINANCES FOR GROWTH

To maintain shrimp farming's growth and profitability, strategic financial planning is essential. To find development prospects and possible obstacles, begin by performing a thorough financial analysis that includes risk assessments, revenue estimates, and cost-benefit analyses. Create a concise business plan that outlines your long- and short-term financial objectives, investment priorities, and performance measures to monitor your advancement.

Whether it's through grants, loans, investment partnerships, or self-financing, find sufficient finance sources to support agricultural expansion. Make well-informed decisions that support the expansion goals of your farm by weighing the interest rates, periods of repayment, and potential impact on cash flow when evaluating financing options.

To reduce financial risk and increase profitability, think about using value-added products, eco-tourism projects, or other forms of income to diversify your revenue streams.

To further optimize resource allocation and guarantee financial stability, put strong financial management procedures into place, such as budgeting, cash flow management, and cost control methods.

Maintaining your shrimp farm's financial stability and promoting sustainable growth will require you to periodically assess financial performance, examine deviations, and make necessary strategy adjustments.

CHAPTER EIGHT

FAQS & TROUBLESHOOTING

TYPICAL PROBLEMS AND DIFFICULTIES IN SHRIMP FARMING

In shrimp farming, maintaining ideal water quality is essential to promoting healthy growth and reducing stress-related problems. Maintaining water pH levels is a typical difficulty because changes can have an impact on the growth and health of shrimp. To remedy this, test the pH of the water regularly using a dependable kit and use natural buffers like crushed limestone or pH regulators to bring the pH within the recommended range of 7.5 to 8.5.

Controlling ammonia and nitrite levels, which can be poisonous to shrimp, is another difficulty. These substances can be broken down by implementing an appropriate filtering system with biological filters. To avoid problems with the quality of water, regular water changes and the monitoring of ammonia and nitrite levels are crucial.

Shrimp are sensitive to temperature changes, thus controlling the temperature is also essential. To keep the water temperature within the ideal range for your variety of shrimp, use heaters or chillers. To avoid oxygen depletion, water must also be properly aerated and oxygenated, particularly in ponds or tanks with a high stock density.

SOLVING ISSUES WITH WATER QUALITY

It's critical to pinpoint the precise problems and take focused action when dealing with water quality issues in shrimp farming. Algal growth or suspended sediments are the main causes of murky water. Water quality can be raised by installing mechanical filters, applying UV sterilizers or algaecides, and clarifying the water.

Elevated ammonia levels are often a cause for concern since they can cause stress and health problems for shrimp. To lower ammonia concentrations, raise water exchange rates, add zeolite or other ammonia-neutralizing agents, and make sure there is enough aeration.

Low oxygen levels can happen, particularly in hot weather or in ponds with a lot of fish. To raise oxygen saturation, increase aeration using paddlewheels, air stones, or aerators. Keep an eye on the oxygen levels and make any adjustments to the aeration to keep the shrimp habitat healthy.

TAKING CARE OF DISEASE EPIDEMICS IN SHRIMP FARMS

If disease outbreaks are not quickly controlled, they can destroy shrimp farms and cause enormous losses. It is essential to have biosecurity measures in place to stop the spread of diseases. This entails stringent hygiene guidelines for agricultural laborers, cleaning of tools and water sources, and quarantine methods for new stock.

Treatment regimens related to common shrimp ailments such as bacterial infections and white spot syndrome virus (WSSV) must be followed. See veterinarians or aquaculture specialists to ensure a precise diagnosis of the illness and the prescription of the right drugs or therapies.

Establishing a routine program for health monitoring makes it possible to identify disease symptoms early and take appropriate action.

Preventing disease also requires maintaining ideal nutrition and water quality. Maintaining a clean environment, sufficient nutrition, and appropriate feeding procedures will help strengthen shrimp's immune systems and reduce their vulnerability to sickness. Keep a regular eye out for any indications of disease or stress in the shrimp behavior and water conditions.

MANAGING VARIATIONS IN DEMAND AND MARKET FLUCTUATIONS

Demand and price swings in the shrimp market can affect farm profitability. Based on consumer preferences and market trends, diversify your product offers to manage market variances. Investigate value-added products to capture niche markets and boost profit margins, such as value-added processed shrimp or organic shrimp.

Creating strategic alliances with eateries, retailers, and seafood wholesalers will assist ensure steady market channels and lessen the effects of market swings. Remain up to date on pricing dynamics, rival strategies, and market trends to make well-informed judgments and modify your output as necessary.

Putting money into marketing and promotional campaigns to showcase the sustainability and great quality of your shrimp products will draw repeat business and set your farm apart from competitors. To increase your market reach and gain access to new consumer categories, look into export options and take part in trade exhibits and industry events.

FREQUENTLY ASKED QUESTIONS (FAQS) REGARDING THE FARMING OF SHRIMP

What infrastructure and equipment are prerequisites for establishing a shrimp farm? Aeration systems, filtration units, feeding systems, heaters or chillers for temperature control, ponds or tanks, and water quality testing kits are examples of essential equipment.

Appropriate site preparation, water supply sources, drainage systems, and safe fencing or nets to keep predators out are all necessary components of infrastructure.

How frequently should a shrimp farm's water quality be examined? A regular testing schedule for characteristics such as pH, ammonia, nitrite, oxygen levels, and temperature should be conducted for water quality, preferably on a daily or at least weekly basis. Maintaining the ideal environment for shrimp growth and health requires regular water quality monitoring.

What are some prevalent illnesses affecting shrimp, and what can be done to avoid them? A: White spot syndrome virus (WSSV), and bacterial, viral, and parasitic infestations are among the common diseases affecting shrimp. Implementing stringent biosecurity protocols, preserving ideal water quality, offering a balanced diet, and doing routine health monitoring are examples of prevention tactics.

CHAPTER NINE

UPCOMING DEVELOPMENTS AND TRENDS

NEW TECHNOLOGY IN SHRIMP AGRICULTURE

Emerging technology has completely changed the way shrimp are farmed, providing effective and long-lasting solutions. The integration of IoT (Internet of Things) devices for real-time temperature, feeding schedules, and water quality monitoring is one noteworthy improvement. By giving farmers access to relevant data, these gadgets help them maximize opportunities and reduce hazards. Additionally, automation has grown in popularity. Automated aerators and feeders simplify operations and cut down on manual labor.

Moreover, genetic engineering has improved overall farm resilience by helping to create disease-resistant shrimp strains. Drone mapping and aerial monitoring have helped to identify areas of possible improvement and concern, which has enhanced agricultural management.

By lowering pollution and resource waste, these technological advancements not only increase production but also support environmental sustainability.

Essentially, incorporating new technologies into shrimp farming increases farm productivity, supports sustainable practices for long-term viability, and gives farmers access to data-driven decision-making tools.

MARKET OPPORTUNITIES AND INDUSTRY TRENDS

Market demands and consumer preferences are changing quickly in the shrimp farming sector, which presents exciting potential for innovation and expansion. Growing awareness of environmental and health issues has led to a notable development in the shrimp industry: a rise in demand for shrimp that is supplied sustainably and organically. Farmers now have more opportunities to implement environmentally beneficial techniques like integrated multi-trophic aquaculture (IMTA) and bio floc systems, which encourage the recycling of natural waste and lessen its negative effects on the environment.

Higher profit margins are also available to producers in specialized markets like gourmet shrimp varieties and value-added goods like convenience meals or snacks made with shrimp. Establishing partnerships with e-commerce platforms and shops enables direct-to-consumer sales, thereby capitalizing on the expanding online market for marine products.

In addition, the focus on certification programs like the Aquaculture Stewardship Council (ASC) accreditation and traceability meets customer demands for ethical sourcing and transparency.

Shrimp farmers can take advantage of these opportunities to broaden their product offerings, increase their market reach, and boost profitability by becoming aware of industry changes and consumer wants.

SUSTAINABLE METHODS FOR SHRIMP FARMING IN THE FUTURE

Due to customer preferences and environmental concerns, sustainability has emerged as a key component of contemporary shrimp farming techniques. Putting sustainable methods into effect requires several tactics, the first of which is managing feed responsibly to reduce waste and maximize nutrition. The use of renewable and locally sourced feed ingredients lessens the need for wild-caught fishmeal and supports the equilibrium of the ecosystem.

In addition, implementing circular economy practices—like repurposing wastewater for biogas generation or irrigation—improves resource efficiency and lessens environmental impact.

By combining shrimp with other complementary species like fish or seaweed, integrated farming systems improve biodiversity and nutrient cycling, resulting in ecosystems that are robust and well-balanced.

Investing in environmentally friendly infrastructure also lowers energy use and greenhouse gas emissions. Examples of such infrastructure include solar-powered equipment and energy-efficient pumps. To further show a dedication to ethical farming techniques, one can embrace sustainable certification requirements and take part in industry activities for water stewardship and habitat conservation.

Shrimp farmers who use sustainable techniques improve their operational efficiency, competitiveness in the market, and long-term sustainability in the changing aquaculture sector in addition to reducing their environmental effect.

INITIATIVES FOR EDUCATION AND TRAINING

To ensure the sustainability of the shrimp farming sector and to advance shrimp farming methods, educational efforts, and training programs are essential. Cooperation amongst government agencies, industry stakeholders, and research institutes promotes knowledge sharing and the development of farming skills.

Best management practices (BMPs) for shrimp farming are the main emphasis of training programs. Topics covered include pond preparation, stocking density management, disease prevention, and water quality management. Farmers are given the tools they need to successfully implement these practices and solve common problems through hands-on training and demonstrations.

In addition, educational programs include information exchange regarding new technologies, sustainable aquaculture practices, and industry trends. For both new and seasoned farmers, there are easily available learning opportunities through webinars, online resources, and mentorship programs.

Participation in educational programs promotes resilience, inventiveness, and ongoing progress within the shrimp farming industry. Farmers may improve their profitability, productivity, and environmental stewardship for a sustainable future by making investments in education and training.

OPPORTUNITIES FOR GLOBAL SHRIMP FARMING GROWTH

Shrimp farming has tremendous potential for international expansion, driven by changing market dynamics, rising demand, and technology breakthroughs. Using international trade agreements to gain market access and broadening product offerings to target specialized markets are two examples of expansion tactics.

For shrimp farming businesses, expanding into new geographic areas with suitable environmental and regulatory environments presents growth opportunities. Joint ventures and strategic alliances open up new markets and distribution avenues in other countries while meeting a range of customer demands and preferences.

Additionally, spending on R&D boosts competitiveness and market differentiation by promoting innovation in value-added processing, product development, and shrimp farming technology.

Engaging in trade shows, industry gatherings, and networking events promotes worldwide exposure, commercial collaborations, and market research.

Moreover, direct-to-consumer sales and worldwide market reach can be achieved by utilizing digital marketing tools and e-commerce platforms in place of conventional distribution channels. Gaining consumer trust and promoting brand loyalty in target markets requires adjusting to local preferences, packaging specifications, and certification norms.

Businesses engaged in shrimp farming can diversify their sources of income, reduce market risk, and promote the global development of aquaculture sustainably by seizing the opportunity to expand internationally.

CHAPTER TEN

PARTICIPATION IN THE COMMUNITY

PARTNERSHIPS AND COOPERATIONS WITH LOCAL COMMUNITIES

Effective alliances and collaborations with nearby communities are critical to the success of shrimp farming operations. Shrimp producers can gain important resources, experience, and support networks by collaborating closely with local stakeholders, including government agencies, non-governmental organizations, and community leaders. These collaborations, which help communities and farmers alike, can take many different forms, from cooperative research initiatives to shared infrastructure development.

Offering training courses and sharing expertise are two ways to work together well. Farmers can give local populations important skills and knowledge by hosting workshops and seminars on disease management, sustainable practices, and shrimp farming techniques.

This raises community involvement and industry support in addition to raising the standard of shrimp farming.

Partnerships might also concentrate on distribution and marketing strategies. Working together with neighborhood companies, cooperatives, and market associations enables shrimp farmers to reach new markets, promote their products more widely, and guarantee reasonable prices. By opening up markets and encouraging local entrepreneurship, these collaborations support the community's economic development.

SOCIAL ACCOUNTABILITY AND ECOLOGICAL GUARDIANSHIP

Shrimp farming requires social responsibility and environmental stewardship to guarantee sustainable methods and reduce adverse effects on the environment and communities. Farmers need to use responsible farming practices, follow rules, and uphold moral principles.

Participation and assistance from the community is one facet of social responsibility. By supporting healthcare and education programs, investing in community projects, and creating job opportunities, shrimp producers may support local development. As a result, there are reciprocal advantages and long-term sustainability between the sector and the community.

Practicing environmental stewardship entails minimizing environmental impact and advancing conservation. This covers appropriate trash disposal, water-saving techniques, and biodiversity preservation. Shrimp growers may reduce pollution, protect natural habitats, and support environmental conservation initiatives by putting into practice environmentally friendly technologies including recirculating aquaculture systems (RAS) and mangrove restoration programs.

OUTREACH PROGRAMS FOR EDUCATION CONCERNING SHRIMP FARMING

Building a knowledgeable workforce and encouraging sustainable shrimp farming practices are two important goals of educational outreach programs. These programs provide information on market trends, environmental protection, and shrimp farming methods to farmers, students, and the general public.

Farmer education is a vital part of educational outreach. Farmers are trained in disease control, water quality management, and shrimp farming best practices through workshops, field demonstrations, and extension services. With this knowledge, farmers may raise their levels of profitability, productivity, and environmental stewardship.

Additionally, curriculum integration and awareness campaigns are used to reach schools and universities as part of educational outreach. These initiatives develop future leaders and supporters of a robust shrimp farming sector by teaching the next generation about the value of sustainable aquaculture, biodiversity conservation, and responsible consumption.

PROMOTING THE CREATION OF JOBS AND LOCAL ECONOMIES

Due to its ability to create jobs, promote economic expansion, and assist small businesses, shrimp farming has a major positive impact on local economies. The industry improves livelihoods and lowers unemployment rates by creating jobs in a variety of industries, including farming, processing, transportation, and marketing.

Shrimp farming contributes to local economies by diversifying and adding value. By processing shrimp to create value-added goods like ready-to-cook meals, snacks, and seafood specialties, farmers can increase the value of their produce. This increases market competitiveness and generates new revenue streams.

Additionally, the production of feed, the manufacture of equipment, and the provision of logistics services are all stimulated by shrimp farming, which has a multiplier effect on the economy. Shrimp farmers support regional growth, business innovation, and economic resilience by cultivating a strong supply chain and market ecology.

DEVELOPING TRUSTING PARTNERSHIPS WITH STAKEHOLDERS

Establishing robust connections with relevant parties is crucial for the sustained prosperity and longevity of the shrimp farming sector. The industry's growth and reputation are shaped by a multitude of stakeholders, including government agencies, regulatory authorities, financial institutions, industry associations, and consumers.

Stakeholder engagement includes, among other things, regulatory compliance and openness. To guarantee product quality, food safety, and market access, shrimp producers must abide by industry rules, environmental regulations, and regulatory standards. Transparent reporting and communication strengthen confidence and trust among stakeholders, improving the standing of the sector.

Furthermore, expanding the market and fostering brand loyalty depends on developing strong relationships with customers. Shrimp farmers may meet customer demand for sustainably sourced and ethically sourced seafood items by differentiating their products in the market and encouraging sustainability certifications, traceability, and quality assurance. This promotes brand loyalty, consumer trust, and market resilience.

www.ingramcontent.com/pod-product-compliance
Lightning Source LLC
Chambersburg PA
CBHW071838210526
45479CB00001B/193